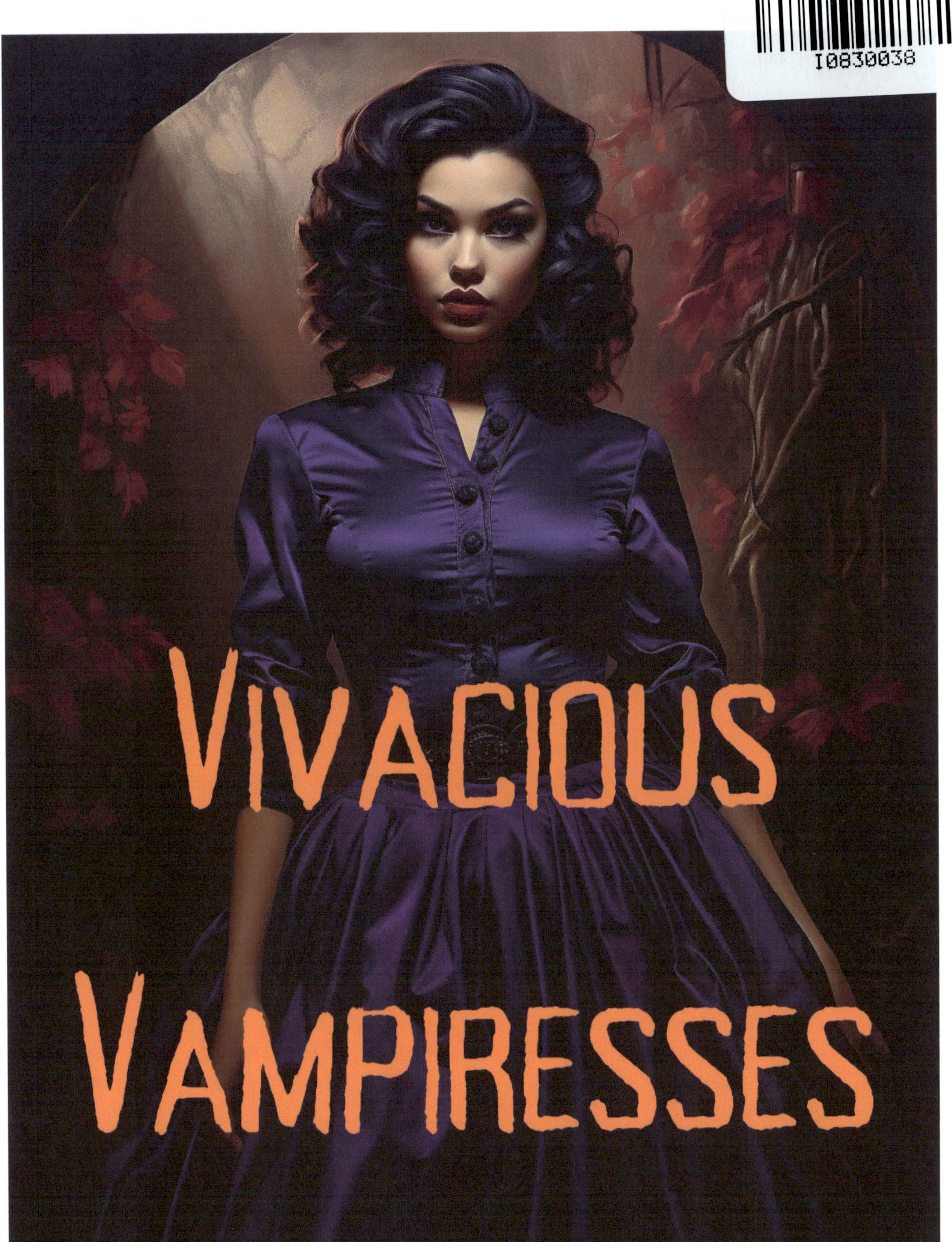

Vivacious
Vampiresses

Introduction

The idea of the female vampire (or vampiress, to use a more old fashioned term) as a beautiful but deadly seductress has been around pretty much as long as literary vampires have, from Carmilla to Vampirella and well into the 21st century.

The descriptive term "vamp", for a seductive woman, is directly taken from vampire, and is allegedly first inspired by the beautiful silent film actress Theda Bara.

Our very fashionable vampiresses are inspired by these film and literary models, along with traditional pin-up art.

These full page, full color illustrations are printed one sided so them may be removed from the book and used as prints, etc. without bleed-through or having to sacrifice an image.

We hope you enjoy them, we enjoyed creating them!